AWAKEN TO THE LIGHT OF SPIRIT

AWAKEN
TO THE
LIGHT OF
SPIRIT

A BOOK OF DEVOTION
TO THE DIVINE MOTHER

JERROLD DONINGTON

Matador
Unit E2 Airfield Business Park,
Harrison Road, Market Harborough,
Leicestershire. LE16 7UL
Tel: 0116 2792299
Email: books@troubador.co.uk
Web: www.troubador.co.uk/matador
Twitter: @matadorbooks

ISBN 978 1803135 632

British Library Cataloguing in Publication Data.
A catalogue record for this book is available from the British Library.

Typeset in 14pt Adobe Garamond Pro by Troubador Publishing Ltd, Leicester, UK

Matador is an imprint of Troubador Publishing Ltd

Dedicated to the Mother and Divine Spirit

This book is also dedicated to the memory of Maria Celeste, who was the eldest daughter of the famed Italian polymath and astronomer Galileo Galilei (1564–1642). Maria was a Catholic nun during her short life (1600–1634). She wrote many letters of devotion to her father which have survived to this day. This correspondence provides an insight into their extraordinary relationship.

BACKGROUND

This book is devoted to the Divine Mother and Spirit. Mother is the supreme goddess and Spirit of life. Spirit is the divine feminine of the primal Creator. This book can be used for healing by meditating on Mother and her sacred story. This is a message of peace and love.

This is the Spirit and Comforter.

The visionary known as 'Jerrold' received a message from Mother through his art. This is a story of Mother that she wishes to be revealed. A summary of this story is presented in this book. This is a revelation that awakens a person to Spirit, including her light and truth.

Awaken to the light of Spirit.

This revelation is dedicated to the Mother and revealed through the pictures in this book. This is spirit art, which is a form of art mediumship or psychic painting. These images have been channelled from Mother and the spiritual realm. However, these images can be enlivened by listening to spiritual music that resonates with this art.

Artists throughout the ages have recorded their spiritual visions. Think of great masters like Michelangelo and Da Vinci. Consider William Blake, who was ridiculed in his life but is now revered. His visions were truly extraordinary and included Adam and Eve. They had a basis in truth. The Mother is also portrayed through many forms of art. But this is not just the religious and Renaissance art of Western civilisation. Sacred art is everywhere.

Music also has a vital role in this renaissance. Sacred music has evolved through the centuries, from Western classical composers to the mystical traditions of India and the East. The world is enriched by music which is a universal language of feeling and passion.

Art can be combined with music to increase its appeal to the spiritual self. So the pictures in this book, when combined with music, may trigger a spiritual awakening. This is an awakening to Spirit and her extraordinary story.

Spirit is the life that we are. We have come from the Spirit.

DEVELOPMENT OF THE ART

Jerrold was called by Spirit in the early 1990s when he entered into a relationship with his soulmate Auriel. Jerrold was also influenced by the New Age renaissance of that time. However, a major spiritual centre in London had already predicted a dramatic shift in his life, when his life would be turned upside down by all these developments.

Auriel encouraged Jerrold to experiment with his art, when he discovered a talent for channelling spiritual pictures. Jerrold was also encouraged by his friend Jack, who was a spiritual therapist. Jack was an expert on the pioneering work of the Swiss psychiatrist Carl Yung, who researched the symbolic language of the unconscious. Through his work with Jack, Jerrold was able to interpret subliminal messages of the unconscious using his art.

Then Auriel passed into spirit and became a guardian angel. With guidance from Auriel, Jerrold took his art across the UK by exhibiting his gift at major holistic shows and the Mind Body Spirit events in London, when Jerrold used his art for readings to his clients.

Through these experiences, it soon became clear that the pictures were 'windows on truth' that Jerrold was receiving from Spirit. Then Jerrold would decipher this truth by interpreting the pictures. However, a much deeper truth had been coded in these images. This is a story of Mother and her divine Spirit.

The revelation in this book is a summary of this story.

HOW TO EXPERIENCE THIS REVELATION

This revelation can be experienced by interpreting the pictures in this book. This can happen through the subconscious with minimal conscious effort. Just let the pictures 'speak' to your intuition. It helps to be relaxed, and possibly in a meditative state, while listening to spiritual music. Sound resonates with truth.

Relax – let the pictures 'speak' to you – while listening to the music of your choice.

An example of a musical playlist is provided in this book. This may help you find the music that you need.

(In other words, this book can be used for meditation and devotion on the Mother and Spirit – whether individually or in a group setting.)

Jerrold Donington
July 2022

THE REVELATION OF ART

A revelation of Spirit is conveyed by these pictures.
This is a universal message of peace and love.

(Don't worry if you don't understand the words. Just focus on the pictures.)

A LIST OF THE PICTURES

1. **The Prophecy.** An angel descends with a prophecy.

2. **The Word.** Creation begins with the Word.

3. **The Spirit.** Creation comes through the Spirit.

4. **Adam and Eve.** The Spirit comes through Eve.

5. **Tree of Life.** The tree is eternal life from Spirit's eternal love.

6. **The Swans.** The soulmates are called by Spirit.

7. **Fire of Love.** This is the divine light of Spirit's eternal love.

8. **The Goddess.** The Goddess comes from Spirit.

9. **The Resurrection.** We are raised by the Spirit.

A revelation of Spirit is conveyed through spirit art.
We have come from the Spirit. This is the Spirit of Mother.

THE REVELATION OF MUSIC

A revelation of music complements the pictures.

The following playlist may help you find the music of your choice. Spiritual music and sound are available from many sources: CDs, DVDs, online streaming, music videos, public concerts, operas and musicals, church and choir, chanting and mantras, personal musicianship, etc.

A PLAYLIST OF MUSIC

1. **Richard Strauss.** Also Sprach Zarathustra

2. **Frédéric Chopin.** Prelude Op 28 'Raindrop'; Berceuse Op 57 in D-flat Major

3. **Devaki Pandit.** Bhagwati Kali Namostute

4. **John Tavener.** The Lamb; Funeral Canticle; Hymn to the Mother of God

5. **Tenebrae.** Miserere; Song for Athene; Hymn to the Cherubim

6. **George Harrison.** Here Comes the Sun; While My Guitar Gently Weeps

7. **Mozart.** Concerto in C major for Flute, Harp and Orchestra

8. **Gabriel Fauré.** Requiem in D minor – In Paradisum

9. **Sonic Safari Productions.** The Master's Breath

10. **The Tibetan Singing Bowls.** Total Zen

11. **Aeoliah.** Whispers Among the Stars; Celestial Sanctuary

12. **Llewellyn.** Archangel Michael

This is an example of a music playlist. This music was available when this book was published. Although music is identified by title and composer, many of its renditions are collaborations between artistes and musicians. Further information about music is generally available from the relevant copyright owners and their agents – and other public sources.

The Prophecy.
An angel descends with a prophecy.

The Word.
Creation begins with the Word.

The Spirit.
Creation comes through the Spirit.

Adam and Eve.
The Spirit comes through Eve.

Tree of Life.

The tree is eternal life from Spirit's eternal love.

The Swans.
The soulmates are called by Spirit.

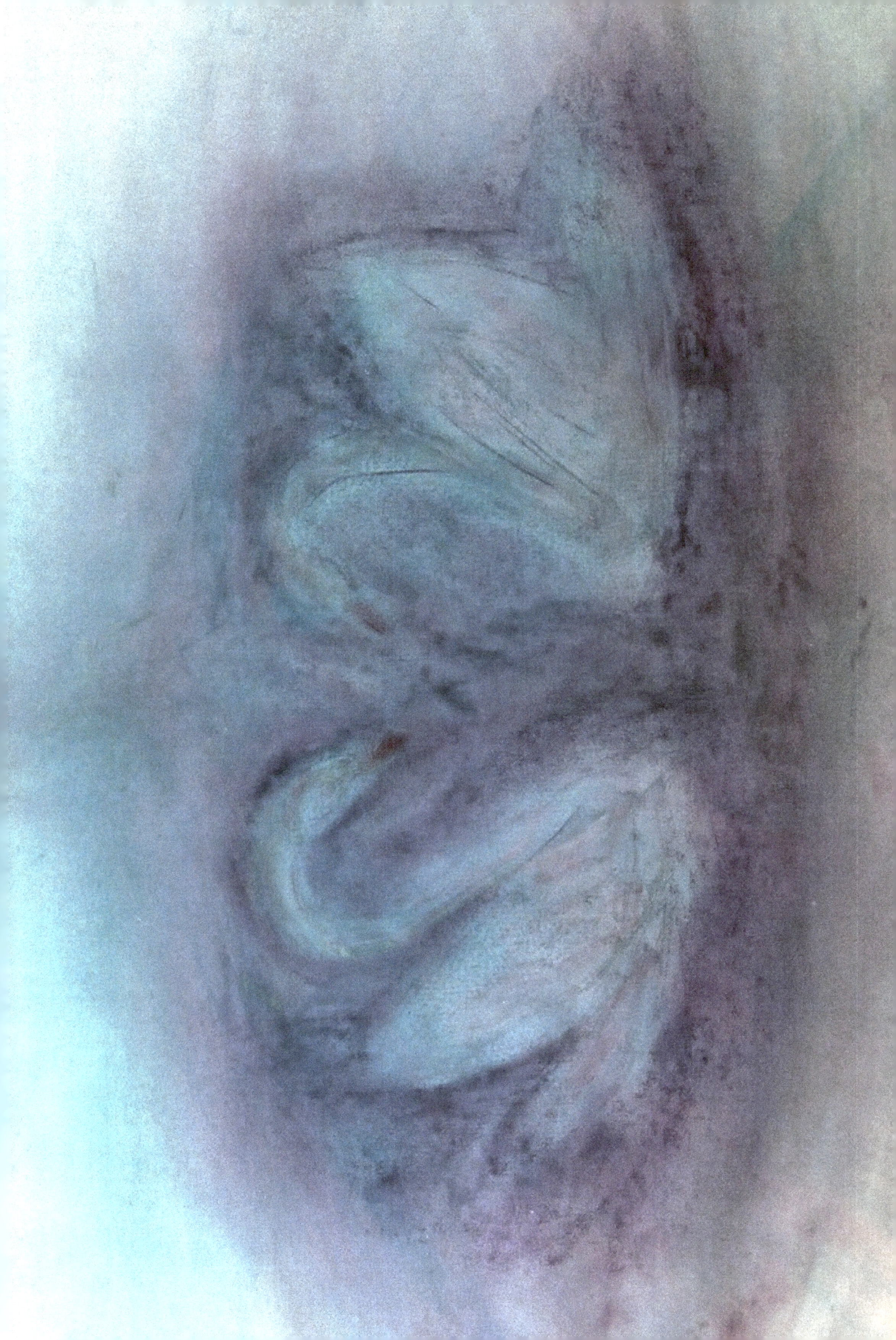

Fire of Love.
This is the divine light of Spirit's eternal love.

The Goddess.
The Goddess comes from Spirit.

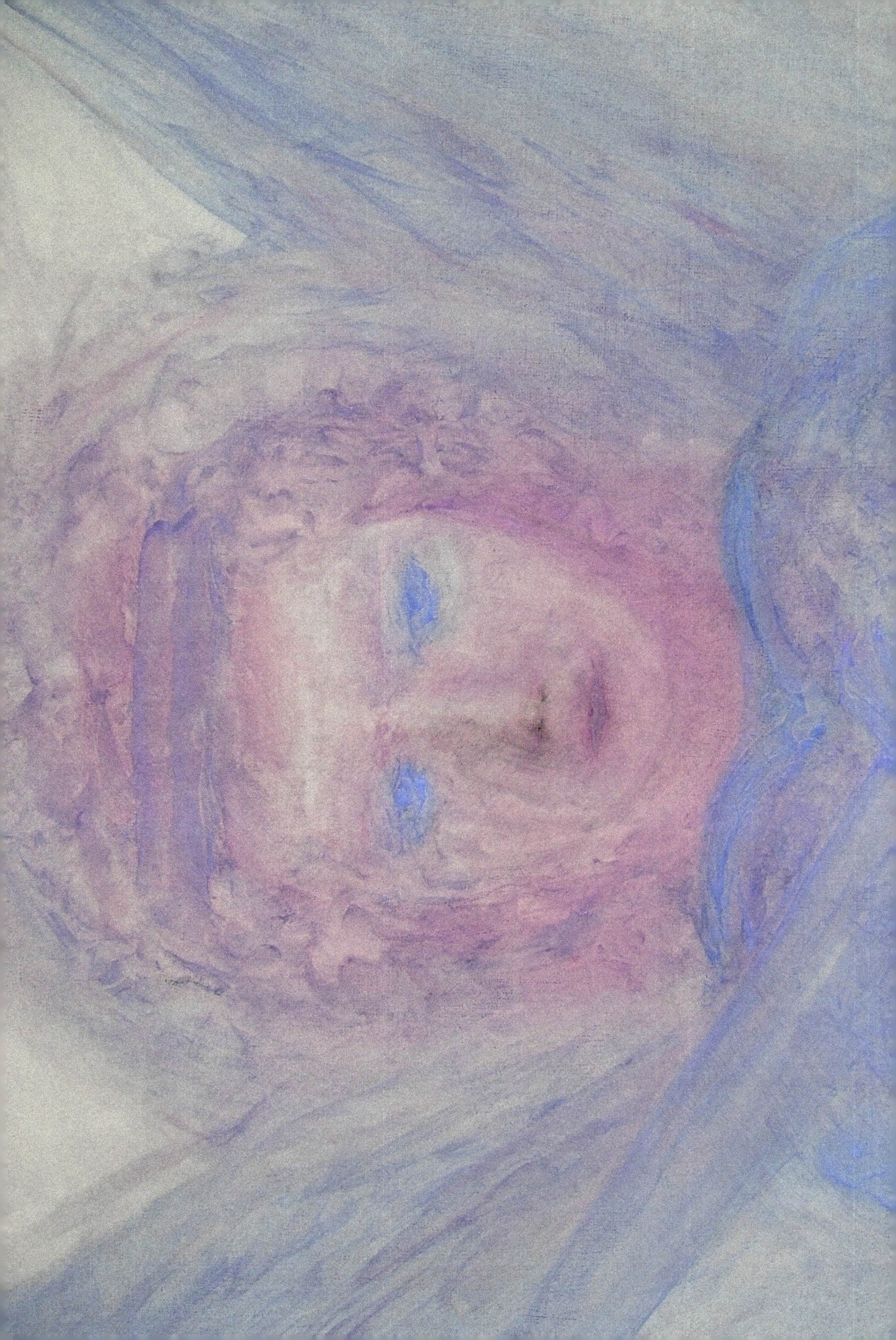

The Resurrection.
We are raised by the Spirit.